Wild Weather
Floods

by Julie Murray

Dash!
LEVELED READERS

3

Dash!
LEVELED READERS

Level 1 – Beginning
Short and simple sentences with familiar words or patterns for children who are beginning to understand how letters and sounds go together.

Level 2 – Emerging
Longer words and sentences with more complex language patterns for readers who are practicing common words and letter sounds.

Level 3 – Transitional
More developed language and vocabulary for readers who are becoming more independent.

abdopublishing.com

Published by Abdo Zoom, a division of ABDO, P.O. Box 398166, Minneapolis, Minnesota 55439.
Copyright © 2018 by Abdo Consulting Group, Inc. International copyrights reserved in all countries.
No part of this book may be reproduced in any form without written permission from the publisher.

Printed in the United States of America, North Mankato, Minnesota.
092017
012018

Photo Credits: iStock, Shutterstock
Production Contributors: Kenny Abdo, Jennie Forsberg, Grace Hansen, John Hansen
Design Contributors: Dorothy Toth, Christina Doffing

Publisher's Cataloging in Publication Data
Names: Murray, Julie, author.
Title: Floods / by Julie Murray.
Description: Minneapolis, Minnesota: Abdo Zoom, 2018. | Series: Wild weather |
    Includes online resource and index.
Identifiers: LCCN 2017939260 | ISBN 9781532120862 (lib.bdg.) | ISBN 9781532121982 (ebook) |
    ISBN 9781532122545 (Read-to-Me ebook)
Subjects: LCSH: Floods--Juvenile literature. | Weather--Juvenile literature. | Environment--Juvenile
    literature.
Classification: DDC 551.489--dc23
LC record available at https://lccn.loc.gov/2017939260

Table of Contents

Floods. 4

Kinds of Floods 10

Flood Protection. 16

More Facts. 22

Glossary 23

Index 24

Online Resources 24

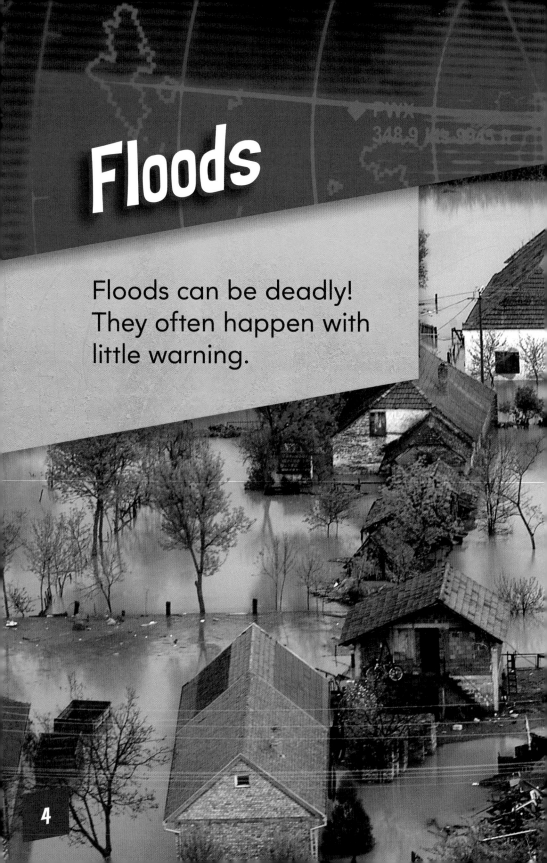

Floods

Floods can be deadly! They often happen with little warning.

Floods occur all over the world. They affect hundreds of thousands of people each year.

Floods can be very powerful. The **raging** waters can carry cars, houses, and people away.

It is dangerous to drive through flooded streets. Cars can be swept away in as little as two feet (0.6 m) of water!

Floods are caused by an overflow of water. This happens when there is too much water for the ground to **absorb**.

Heavy rain or melting snow can cause floods. Floods also occur from storms that make sea levels rise, like a hurricane.

Kinds of Floods

1: Fluvial Flood
2: Coastal Flood
3: Flash Flood

There are three kinds of floods:
fluvial, coastal, and flash.

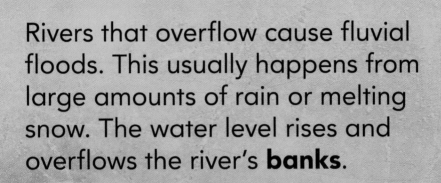

Rivers that overflow cause fluvial floods. This usually happens from large amounts of rain or melting snow. The water level rises and overflows the river's **banks**.

Coastal floods are caused by a rise in sea level. This usually happens from a storm, like a hurricane.

The rise in sea level is caused by a storm surge. Strong winds push the water inland. This causes flooding along the coastline.

Flash floods happen quickly.
There is usually very little
warning.

They are caused by heavy rains or a break in a dam or levee. Most flood deaths occur from flash floods.

Flood Protection

There are ways to protect areas from flooding. Levees are large mounds of dirt.

They can be man-made or occur naturally. They help keep rising water at bay.

Many cities build floodwalls.
These are artificial walls that
protect large areas from
rising water.

Sandbags work well to protect smaller areas. Some people put sandbags around their homes.

Getting to higher ground is important in floods. Many coastal cities have **evacuation** routes.

These routes are the quickest way to safer ground. Be sure to have a plan in case a flood happens in your area. It could save your life!

- The word "flood" comes from an old English word that means, "a flowing of water, river, or sea."

- Floods cause around $6 billion in damage in the U.S. each year.

- Hurricane Katrina, in 2005, caused $81 billion in damage. It was responsible for 1,833 deaths. About 80% of New Orleans was flooded.

Glossary

absorb – to take in or soak up.

bank – the ground at the edge of a river or stream.

evacuation – the removal of people from an endangered place.

raging – continuing with great force or intensity.

Index

cause 8, 11, 12, 14, 15

coastal flood 12, 13

damage 6, 7

danger 7, 15

flash flood 10, 14, 15

floodwall 18

fluvial flood 10, 11

levee 15, 16

prevention 16, 17, 18, 19

safety 20, 21

sandbags 19

Online Resources

Booklinks
NONFICTION NETWORK
FREE! ONLINE NONFICTION RESOURCES

To learn more about floods, please visit **abdobooklinks.com**. These links are routinely monitored and updated to provide the most current information available.